To Seek and To Save
workbook

winning and building
committed followers
of Jesus Christ

Paul Chappell

First published in 1996 by Striving Together Publications, a
ministry of Lancaster Baptist Church, Lancaster, CA 93535.
Striving Together Publications is committed to providing tried,
trusted, and proven books that will further equip local churches
to carry out the Great Commission. Your comments and
suggestions are valued.

Striving Together Publications
4020 E. Lancaster Blvd.
Lancaster, CA 93535
800.201.7748

Cover design by Jeremy Lofgren
Layout by Craig Parker
Edited by Maggie Ruhl
Special thanks to our proofreaders.

ISBN 1-59894-018-X

Printed in the United States of America

Table of Contents

.

Principles of Soul Winning

Introduction: _____
_____
_____

I. The _mandate_ of Soul Winning

"Go ye therefore, and teach all nations, baptizing them in the name of the Father, and of the Son, and of the Holy Ghost: Teaching them to observe all things whatsoever I have commanded you: and, lo, I am with you alway, even unto the end of the world. Amen."
—MATTHEW 28:19–20

A. An _Authorizing_ _mandate_

1. Soul winning is not a _Spiritual_ gift.

2. Christians must operate on the foundation of the Lord's _Soveign_ authority.

B. An _Active_ _mandate_

"And he said unto them, Go ye into all the world, and preach the gospel to every creature."—MARK 16:15

"Go, stand and speak in the temple to the people all the words of this life."—ACTS 5:20

• The only way to fulfill the mandate is to "go" and talk to someone about Christ.

C. An _____ _____

Acts 2:41

- Absolute means "perfect in quality and nature, or complete."
    1. _Go_ wins souls to Christ.
    2. _Baptize_ them.
    3. _Teach_ them God's Word.

D. An _Accompanied mandate_

- Christ promises to each soul winner—"...lo, I am with you alway.."(Matthew 28:20).

Jeremiah 17:10 – He knows one motives.

II. The _motive_ of Soul Winning

A. The Right _motives_

- To please and glorify the Lord

B. Christ—Our _example_

"For the Son of man is come to seek and to save that which was lost."—LUKE 19:10

1. Christ was motivated by the brevity of _time_ .

2. Christ was motivated by the desire to _please_ His Father.

Matt 4:19 Follow me / make to be fishers of men

III. The _ministry_ of a Soul Winner

A. To be effective—be a _faithful_ Christian.

"And he saith unto them, Follow me, and I will make you fishers of men."—Matthew 4:19

B. To be effective—be a _filled_

Christian.

"But ye shall receive power, after that the Holy Ghost is come upon you: and ye shall be witnesses unto me both in Jerusalem, and in all Judaea, and in Samaria, and unto the uttermost part of the earth."—Acts 1:8

"Howbeit when he, the Spirit of truth, is come, he will guide you into all truth: for he shall not speak of himself; but whatsoever he shall hear, that shall he speak: and he will shew you things to come. He shall glorify me: for he shall receive of mine, and shall shew it unto you."—John 16:13–14

C. To be effective—be a _empowered / spirit filled_

Witness. _faithful_

"And how I kept back nothing that was profitable unto you, but have shewed you, and have taught you publickly, and from house to house."—Acts 20:20

"They that sow in tears shall reap in joy. He that goeth forth and weepeth, bearing precious seed, shall doubtless come again with rejoicing, bringing his sheaves with him."—Psalm 126:5–6

Only good can come out of this!

Preparation for Soul Winning

Introduction: _Know what it takes!_

I. _Salvation_ Day

"But we all, with open face beholding as in a glass the glory of the Lord, are changed into the same image from glory to glory, even as by the Spirit of the Lord. Therefore seeing we have this ministry, as we have received mercy, we faint not."—2 CORINTHIANS 3:18–4:1

"Therefore if any man be in Christ, he is a new creature: old things are passed away; behold, all things are become new."—2 CORINTHIANS 5:17

"Know ye not that ye are the temple of God, and that the Spirit of God dwelleth in you?"—1 CORINTHIANS 3:16

"Now therefore ye are no more strangers and foreigners, but fellowcitizens with the saints, and of the household of God."—EPHESIANS 2:19

A. The _transmition_ of Spiritual _truth_
"And the things that thou hast heard of me among many witnesses, the same commit thou to faithful men, who shall be able to teach others also."
—2 TIMOTHY 2:2

St John 4:5

9

1. "*Thou*"—indicates the _impurtance_ of the individual.

2. "*Me*"—indicates the _personal_ nature of the contact.

3. "*Commit*"—transmitting _truth_ to a receiver.

4. "*Faithful men*"—responsible for _teaching_ the truth to others.

5. "*Teach others also*"—the spiritual transmission begins to _multiply_.

B. A _Change_ of Mind

"*And I said, What shall I do, Lord? And the Lord said unto me, Arise, and go into Damascus; and there it shall be told thee of all things which are appointed for thee to do.*"—ACTS 22:10

1. Salvation is evidenced by a _desire_ to please the _Lord_.

2. Salvation is evidenced by a _____ to serve the Lord _____.

C. A Truthful _purpose_ in Life

•   With the gift of _____ comes responsibility.

"*Who hath saved us, and called us with an holy calling, not according to our works, but according to his own purpose and grace, which was given us in Christ Jesus before the world began.*"—2 TIMOTHY 1:9

"*For even hereunto were ye called: because Christ also suffered for us, leaving us an example, that ye should follow his steps.*"—1 PETER 2:21

II. Spiritual _prerequisites_

• The primary prerequisite for soul winning is that the soul winner be _saved_.

A. A Proper Life's _objective_

• The Christian's objective should be _parallel_ to that which God has set forth in the _Scriptures_.

"But seek ye first the kingdom of God, and his righteousness; and all these things shall be added unto you."—MATTHEW 6:33

B. Willing to _pay_ a Price

"Thou therefore endure hardness, as a good soldier of Jesus Christ. No man that warreth entangleth himself with the affairs of this life; that he may please him who hath chosen him to be a soldier."
—2 TIMOTHY 2:3–4

C. A _Love_ for God's Word

"Thy words were found, and I did eat them; and thy word was unto me the joy and rejoicing of mine heart: for I am called by thy name, O LORD God of hosts."—JEREMIAH 15:16

D. A _Servants_ Heart

"But it shall not be so among you: but whosoever will be great among you, let him be your minister; And whosoever will be chief among you, let him be your servant: Even as the Son of man came not to be ministered unto, but to minister, and to give his life a ransom for many."—MATTHEW 20:26–28

E. Putting No _Confidence_ **in the** _flesh_

"*But we had the sentence of death in ourselves, that we should not trust in ourselves, but in God which raiseth the dead.*"—2 Corinthians 1:9

"*Herein is love, not that we loved God, but that he loved us, and sent his Son to be the propitiation for our sins. Beloved, if God so loved us, we ought also to love one another.*"—1 John 4:10–11

God Blesses my Confidence in him!

- The soul winner should have a genuine love for people.

F. Avoiding _bitterness_

"*Looking diligently lest any man fail of the grace of God; lest any root of bitterness springing up trouble you, and thereby many be defiled.*"—Hebrews 12:15

G. Leading a _disciplined_ **Life**

"*Know ye not that they which run in a race run all, but one receiveth the prize? So run, that ye may obtain. And every man that striveth for the mastery is temperate in all things. Now they do it to obtain a corruptible crown; but we an incorruptible. I therefore so run, not as uncertainly; so fight I, not as one that beateth the air: But I keep under my body, and bring it into subjection: lest that by any means, when I have preached to others, I myself should be a castaway.*"—1 Corinthians 9:24–27

These prerequisites are not rules; rather they reflect the attitude of a Spirit-filled soul winner.

III. The _____*Cost*_____ of Soul Winning

- Soul winning is an opportunity to learn to _____ on the infinite _____ of God.

A. _____ — _____

   1. The willingness to _____ all in order to gain everything.

> *"And he said to them all, If any man will come after me, let him deny himself, and take up his cross daily, and follow me. For whosoever will save his life shall lose it: but whosoever will lose his life for my sake, the same shall save it."*
> —LUKE 9:23–24

> *"No man can serve two masters: for either he will hate the one, and love the other; or else he will hold to the one, and despise the other. Ye cannot serve God and mammon. Therefore I say unto you, Take no thought for your life, what ye shall eat, or what ye shall drink; nor yet for your body, what ye shall put on. Is not the life more than meat, and the body than raiment?"*
> —MATTHEW 6:24–25

   2. The soul winner must be willing to _____ his faith, realizing that those without Christ are captives of Satan and that only the Gospel can set them free.

> *"Thou therefore, my son, be strong in the grace that is in Christ Jesus. And the things that thou hast heard of me among many witnesses, the*

same commit thou to faithful men, who shall be able to teach others also."—2 TIMOTHY 2:1–2

3. The unsaved man will be moved by the testimony of a soul winner who _____ the price of self-sacrifice.

B. _____ _____

• Because a soul winner is stepping forward as an example to the world, lack of personal _____ could be a major hindrance for the cause of Christ.

"Thou therefore endure hardness, as a good soldier of Jesus Christ. No man that warreth entangleth himself with the affairs of this life; that he may please him who hath chosen him to be a soldier."
—2 TIMOTHY 2:3–4

C. _____ _____

1. When society becomes intolerant of Christianity, _____ always results.

    "Wherein I suffer trouble, as an evildoer, even unto bonds; but the word of God is not bound."
    —2 TIMOTHY 2:9

2. No soul winner should seek persecution or trouble in order to gain God's approval, but rather he should _____ and saturate himself in God's Word.

    "Study to shew thyself approved unto God, a workman that needeth not to be ashamed, rightly dividing the word of truth."—2 TIMOTHY 2:15

D. _____   _____

    1.   Because of the need to be ready to give an answer to all the pertinent _____, soul winners must become diligent students of the Word of God.

        "For I determined not to know any thing among you, save Jesus Christ, and him crucified."
        —1 CORINTHIANS 2:2

    2.   A sincere soul winner has a _____ heart and is willing to be a _____ to all men in order to win some for Christ.

        "And the servant of the Lord must not strive; but be gentle unto all men, apt to teach, patient."
        —2 TIMOTHY 2:24

E. _____   _____

    1.   It is the Holy Spirit of God who will ultimately do the _____ through the Word of God.

        "So then faith cometh by hearing, and hearing by the word of God."—ROMANS 10:17

    2.   It is the Holy Spirit of God who _____ the believer.

        "And be not drunk with wine, wherein is excess; but be filled with the Spirit."—EPHESIANS 5:18

    3.   It is the Holy Spirit of God who _____ the soul winner in the truth of God's Word.

        "Howbeit when he, the Spirit of truth, is come, he will guide you into all truth: for he shall not

speak of himself; but whatsoever he shall hear, that shall he speak: and he will shew you things to come. He shall glorify me: for he shall receive of mine, and shall shew it unto you."—JOHN 16:13–14

- Hudson Taylor once said, "It is possible to move men, through God, by prayer alone."

Principles of the Gospel

Introduction: _____

_____

_____

I. Man's _____

A. *All have* _____

- Before an individual can be saved…

1. He must understand his _____ for a
   _____.

   "As it is written, There is none righteous, no, not one."—ROMANS 3:10

   "For all have sinned, and come short of the glory of God."—ROMANS 3:23

   "For there is not a just man upon earth, that doeth good, and sinneth not."—ECCLESIASTES 7:20

   "But we are all as an unclean thing, and all our righteousnesses are as filthy rags; and we all do fade as a leaf; and our iniquities, like the wind, have taken us away."—ISAIAH 64:6

2. He must understand that he is a _____
   because all men are born in _____.
   "Wherefore, as by one man sin entered into the world, and death by sin; and so death passed upon all men, for that all have sinned."
   —ROMANS 5:12

B. Sin _____ man from God

- The _____ of sin is separation from God.

"Therefore as by the offence of one judgment came upon all men to condemnation; even so by the righteousness of one the free gift came upon all men unto justification of life."—ROMANS 5:18

C. The Sinner is _____ to Hell

"He that believeth on him is not condemned: but he that believeth not is condemned already, because he hath not believed in the name of the only begotten Son of God."—JOHN 3:18

"He that believeth on the Son hath everlasting life: and he that believeth not the Son shall not see life; but the wrath of God abideth on him."—JOHN 3:36

"For the wages of sin is death; but the gift of God is eternal life through Jesus Christ our Lord."
—ROMANS 6:23

- Man's sinful nature separates him from God and separation leads to eternal _____.

II. God's _____

"Jesus said unto her, I am the resurrection, and the life: he that believeth in me, though he were dead, yet shall he live: And whosoever liveth and believeth in me shall never die. Believest thou this?"—JOHN 11:25–26

"I am the door: by me if any man enter in, he shall be saved, and shall go in and out, and find pasture."
—JOHN 10:9

A. The Person of _____—His _____

1. Christ is called _____.

   "And we know that the Son of God is come, and hath given us an understanding, that we may know him that is true, and we are in him that is true, even in his Son Jesus Christ. This is the true God, and eternal life."—1 JOHN 5:20

   "For in him dwelleth all the fulness of the Godhead bodily."—COLOSSIANS 2:9

   "And the Word was made flesh, and dwelt among us, (and we beheld his glory, the glory as of the only begotten of the Father,) full of grace and truth."—JOHN 1:14

2. Christ is pre-_____.

   "In the beginning was the Word, and the Word was with God, and the Word was God."—JOHN 1:1

   "In the beginning God created the heaven and the earth."—GENESIS 1:1

   "And now, O Father, glorify thou me with thine own self with the glory which I had with thee before the world was."—JOHN 17:5

3. Christ is self-_____ and has life-giving power.

"For as the Father raiseth up the dead, and quickeneth them; even so the Son quickeneth whom he will."—JOHN 5:21

"For as the Father hath life in himself; so hath he given to the Son to have life in himself."—JOHN 5:26

4. Christ is _____.
    "And Jesus came and spake unto them, saying, All power is given unto me in heaven and in earth."—MATTHEW 28:18

    "I am he that liveth, and was dead; and, behold, I am alive for evermore, Amen; and have the keys of hell and of death."—REVELATION 1:18

    "As thou hast given him power over all flesh, that he should give eternal life to as many as thou hast given him."—JOHN 17:2

5. Christ is _____.
    "Now are we sure that thou knowest all things, and needest not that any man should ask thee: by this we believe that thou camest forth from God."—JOHN 16:30

    "But Jesus did not commit himself unto them, because he knew all men."—JOHN 2:24

    "In whom are hid all the treasures of wisdom and knowledge."—COLOSSIANS 2:3

6. Christ is _____.

"For where two or three are gathered together in my name, there am I in the midst of them."
—Matthew 18:20

"Teaching them to observe all things whatsoever I have commanded you: and, lo, I am with you alway, even unto the end of the world. Amen."
—Matthew 28:20

"Which is his body, the fulness of him that filleth all in all."—Ephesians 1:23

7. Divine offices are ascribed to _____.

    a. Christ is our _____.
        "All things were made by him; and without him was not any thing made that was made."—John 1:3

        "And, Thou, Lord, in the beginning hast laid the foundation of the earth; and the heavens are the works of thine hands."—Hebrews 1:10

    b. Christ has power to _____ sins.
        "And he said unto her, Thy sins are forgiven."
        —Luke 7:48

    c. Christ has power over _____.
        "Jesus said unto her, I am the resurrection, and the life: he that believeth in me, though he were dead, yet shall he live."—John 11:25

B. The_____ of Christ—His Cross

•   Christ's work at Calvary was a _____ of redemption.

"But God commendeth his love toward us, in that, while we were yet sinners, Christ died for us."
—ROMANS 5:8

"The next day John seeth Jesus coming unto him, and saith, Behold the Lamb of God, which taketh away the sin of the world."—JOHN 1:29

"For I delivered unto you first of all that which I also received, how that Christ died for our sins according to the scriptures; And that he was buried, and that he rose again the third day according to the scriptures."—1 CORINTHIANS 15:3–4

III. Man's _____

A. _____ *the Gospel*
"Testifying both to the Jews, and also to the Greeks, repentance toward God, and faith toward our Lord Jesus Christ."—ACTS 20:21

- In the realm of salvation there is a close relationship between _____ and

   _____.

   1. _____

      - Definition—to turn around and go in the opposite direction, or to _____ one's mind.

      - The sinner repents when he realizes he is a sinner before God, that he deserves God's righteous judgment.

2. _____

- Definition—turning to and _____ in Jesus Christ.

- Believing that Jesus Christ is the only means by which we are to be forgiven and to receive eternal life.

B. Exercising _____ Faith

"But without faith it is impossible to please him: for he that cometh to God must believe that he is, and that he is a rewarder of them that diligently seek him."—HEBREWS 11:6

1. Genuine faith is claiming by personal

   _____.

   "But as many as received him, to them gave he power to become the sons of God, even to them that believe on his name: Which were born, not of blood, nor of the will of the flesh, nor of the will of man, but of God."—JOHN 1:12–13

2. Genuine faith involves _____ in Christ alone.

   - Faith involves…

     a. Trusting alone in Jesus

     b. Relying solely on Jesus

     c. Grasping onto Jesus alone

     d. Claiming only Jesus

     e. Seizing only Jesus

     f. Believing only in Jesus

Presenting the Gospel

Introduction: _____
_____
_____

I.   The _____, the First Few Words

A. _____ *Yourself*

- Approach the door with a spirit of optimism and expectation.

- Sample introduction:

  "Mr. Jones? Hello, my name is _____, and this is _____. We are from _____ Church. We are happy to have _____ as part of our children's Sunday school class. We would love to be able to take a few minutes and tell you a little about our Sunday school program. Could you spare a few moments for us to tell you a few things about the program?

  1. Find out the _____ name and use it.

  2. _____ your own name clearly, as well as your partner's name.

  3. State the name of your _____ clearly.

     - Being from a Baptist church may relieve the person's fear of cult association.

4. State the _____ for the visit.

5. Ask the listener for a few _____ of his time.

B. Starting the _____

1. After the introduction, there is usually a need to talk _____ for a moment.

2. Be _____ interested in people and their lives.

3. Encourage the person to _____ and in turn, learn to _____.

C. Continuing the _____

1. Lead the discussion toward _____ things.

2. Find out the person's _____ background.

3. Be careful not to _____ or jump quickly to conclusions.

4. Listen intently and remember _____ of the person's background to help later in the discussion.

5. Some questions you may want to ask while continuing the discussion:

   a. *How did you first* _____ *about the church?*

   b. *Do you have any* _____ *about the church?*

II. Turning the _____ toward Christ

A. The Three _____

- Three statements to transition from generalities to the specific truth of Christ:

1. _____—any church involvement.

   - Statement 1: "Mr. Jones, I think it is really good that you are sending your child to Sunday school, and I am also glad to know that you have a religious background."

2. _____—yourself with the individual.

   - Statement 2: "It is very important that each of us attend church and that our children attend Sunday school. I have always enjoyed church attendance."

3. _____—any erroneous thought that religion can save.

   - Statement 3: "However, church attendance and religion in themselves have never given salvation to anyone."

4. Give a brief personal _____.

   a. *Reaffirm the three Cs.*

   b. *Tell about your condition before being saved.*

   c. *Describe your discovery that religion couldn't save you.*

   d. *Include how you heard of God's plan of salvation.*

    e. *Tell how you accepted Christ as Saviour.*

    f. *State that you are sure that Christ is the only way to Heaven.*

    g. *Tell how Christ has made a wonderful difference in your life.*

B. Important _____

1. If you were to die today, are you 100% sure that you would go to Heaven?

2. If he says no, ask…"May I take a few moments to show you from the Scriptures how you can know for sure you are going to Heaven?"

3. If he says yes, ask…"May I ask how you know that you are on your way to Heaven?"

C. The Heart of the _____

1. Reaching souls for Christ is the purpose for which the soul winner has made great _____ and _____.

2. Reaching souls for Christ can only be accomplished by the presentation of the Gospel plan of salvation.

D. A Suggested _____

1. Realize there is none _____.
   "As it is written, There is none righteous, no, not one."—ROMANS 3:10

   - Explain that all men have a sin nature and that sin separates man from God and from His glory.

2. See yourself as a _____.
   "For all have sinned, and come short of the glory of God."—ROMANS 3:23

   "Wherefore, as by one man sin entered into the world, and death by sin; and so death passed upon all men, for that all have sinned."
   —ROMANS 5:12

3. Notice God's _____ on sin.
   "For the wages of sin is death; but the gift of God is eternal life through Jesus Christ our Lord."
   —ROMANS 6:23

4. Realize that _____ died for _____.
   "But God commendeth his love toward us, in that, while we were yet sinners, Christ died for us."—ROMANS 5:8

   • Use an illustration on the words _____ and _____.

   a. _____—*"deserving payment"*

      • *Illustration—paycheck as payment for work*

   b. _____— *"has already been paid for"*

      • *Illustration—relating to a birthday or Christmas gift*

5. _____ Salvation
   "That if thou shalt confess with thy mouth the Lord Jesus, and shalt believe in thine heart that God hath raised him from the dead, thou shalt be saved. For with the heart man believeth unto righteousness; and with the mouth confession

*is made unto salvation. For the scripture
saith, Whosoever believeth on him shall not be
ashamed."*—ROMANS 10:9–11

*"For God so loved the world, that he gave his only
begotten Son, that whosoever believeth in him
should not perish, but have everlasting life."*
—JOHN 3:16

6. _____ God at His _____.
"For whosoever shall call upon the name of the
Lord shall be saved."—ROMANS 10:13

- Stress confessing with *their* mouth and
  believing in their heart.

7. Review the three basic principles.

   a. *All men are _____ and sin
   separates men from God.*

   b. *Jesus _____ to forgive men's sins.*

   c. *If an individual will admit his need for
   Christ (because of sin) and will place his
   _____ in Him alone for salvation,
   he will be _____.*

- It is vital that the prospect *completely
  understands* the Scriptures and truths
  presented before praying and accepting
  Jesus as Saviour.

III. Leading to a _____

A. *Three effective _____ to ask:*

1. Question 1: "Mr. Jones, do you believe that you are a _____, separated from _____, and without the ability to save yourself?"

2. Question 2: "Do you believe that Jesus, God's Son, shed His blood to _____ for your sin?"

3. Question 3: "Would there be anything that would stop you from praying and _____ Jesus Christ as your Saviour today?"

B. When a person digs in and becomes determined not to make a decision for Christ, leave a Gospel tract with your phone number and make him feel _____ to call your home when he is ready to _____ Christ as Saviour.

C. When a prospect agrees that there is nothing that would stand in the way of receiving Christ, review the following verses:

"That if thou shalt confess with thy mouth the Lord Jesus, and shalt believe in thine heart that God hath raised him from the dead, thou shalt be saved. For with the heart man believeth unto righteousness; and with the mouth confession is made unto salvation."—ROMANS 10:9–10

"For whosoever shall call upon the name of the Lord shall be saved."—ROMANS 10:13

"Whosoever therefore shall confess me before men, him will I confess also before my Father which is in heaven."—MATTHEW 10:32

D. **After _____ covering the need to pray and accept Christ, say, "Mr. Jones, I would like to encourage you to pray and ask Christ to forgive your sins and become your _____."**

E. **At the conclusion of the prospect's prayer, pray a prayer of _____ to the Lord for the wonderful _____.**

IV. Leaving a New _____ with _____

- The moment an individual accepts Christ as his personal Saviour, Satan will begin to bring _____ and _____ into his life.
- The soul winner's responsibility is to give scriptural support and encouragement to _____ his faith in the Lord.

A. *Providing Scriptural Assurance of Salvation*
"And this is the record, that God hath given to us eternal life, and this life is in his Son. He that hath the Son hath life; and he that hath not the Son of God hath not life. These things have I written unto you that believe on the name of the Son of God; that ye may know that ye have eternal life, and that ye may believe on the name of the Son of God."
—1 JOHN 5:11–13

"For by grace are ye saved through faith; and that not of yourselves: it is the gift of God: Not of works, lest any man should boast."—EPHESIANS 2:8–9

"But as many as received him, to them gave he power to become the sons of God, even to them that believe on his name."—JOHN 1:12

- You may want to ask, "Based upon the Scriptures, if your life ended today, where would you spend eternity?"

B. Providing Scriptural Warnings from False Teachers

"As ye have therefore received Christ Jesus the Lord, so walk ye in him: Rooted and built up in him, and stablished in the faith, as ye have been taught, abounding therein with thanksgiving. Beware lest any man spoil you through philosophy and vain deceit, after the tradition of men, after the rudiments of the world, and not after Christ."—COLOSSIANS 2:6–8

C. Provide a Written Record of What Took Place

- Write down the _____ of the new convert's salvation in his Bible or on a Gospel tract.

"Verily, verily, I say unto you, He that heareth my word, and believeth on him that sent me, hath everlasting life, and shall not come into condemnation; but is passed from death unto life."—JOHN 5:24

Procedures in Soul Winning

Introduction: _____

_____

_____

- The first priority of soul winning is the preparation of the _____.

- The next priority is to remember every soul winner is an _____ or _____ for Christ.

I. _____

A. *Manners and Etiquette*

1. Never cut across a _____—use the _____.

2. When knocking at the door, stand on the _____ side so when the resident opens the door, the soul winner speaking is the one he _____.

3. Give a polite, _____ introduction of yourself, your partner, and your _____.

4. Avoid getting too close to the resident's " _____ _____."

5. Apologize if a _____ is interrupted or the resident is in bed clothes.

6. Avoid _____ the prospect in the middle of a statement. Be patient!

7. Do not _____ or display a prideful spirit.

8. Possess a _____ heart.

B. The Silent Partner

1. Remain _____ in what the soul winner is saying and be _____ to offer input if asked.

2. Minimize _____.

3. Dedicate yourself to _____.

- A partner's _____ can go a long way in winning the spiritual battle for the prospect's soul.

II. _____ of _____

A. The Christian

1. A Christian must remember he is _____ Christ daily.

2. The unsaved world cannot look at a Christian's _____ _____ condition; therefore, it is imperative that his outward appearance is becoming of a Christian.

   "Therefore if any man be in Christ, he is a new creature: old things are passed away; behold, all things are become new."—2 CORINTHIANS 5:17

3. A soul winner's appearance should reflect the _____ of God.

   "For even hereunto were ye called: because Christ also suffered for us, leaving us an example, that ye should follow his steps."—1 PETER 2:21

B. _____ *Tips for* _____

   1. Everyone

- *Clothing should be pressed, clean and matching.*

   2. Ladies

- *Ladies should wear a knee-length skirt or dress.*

- *Clothing should never be tight, clingy or revealing.*

   3. Men

- *Hair should be cut and combed properly. (Above the ears)*

- *Shoes should be shined.*

- *Men should wear a tie, sport coat and dress shoes.*

III. _____ in Soul Winning

A. *Unfamiliar Terminology*

   1. Words used in church: "We're out _____ tonight."

- *Recommended substitute: "We're out _____ others about Jesus Christ."*

   2. Words used in church: "Has anyone ever told you how to be _____?"

- *Recommended substitute: "Has anyone ever told you how to _____ Christ as your personal Saviour and know that you are on your way to Heaven?"*

B. Words to Avoid

1. "Have you ever been _____ again?"

   • *Recommended substitute: "Have you ever recognized that you were separated from God and prayed to _____ Jesus Christ as your Saviour?"*

2. "Are you a _____?"

   • *Recommended substitute: "Are you sure that you are on your way to _____?"*

IV. The Soul Winning _____

A. Important reasons for taking a partner:

1. Accountability

   • *Having a _____ soul winning partner will help you remain faithful, because you are _____ to another person.*

2. Safety

   • *Oftentimes our calls may take us to areas which are known for high crime rate.*

3. Protection against slander

   • *The devil will use any _____ in the book to ruin a faithful servant of Christ.*

B. Specific direction for the soul winning partner

1. Be the silent partner

- *If two people are attempting to _____ the direction of the conversation, the prospect will be lost in _____.*

2. Pray

   - *The greatest help the soul winning partner can offer is to _____ that the Holy Spirit would do a work in the heart of the prospect.*

3. Prevent Distractions

   - *During the course of a soul winning visit, Satan will send many _____ to turn the attention away from God's _____.*

Discipleship: Proper Follow-Up

Introduction: _____

_____

_____

I. _____ : First Follow-Up Visit

A. *Christ's Promise to Keep Us*

- One can _____ that he has eternal life because Jesus Christ is powerful enough to keep him until the day of His return.

"He that believeth on the Son of God hath the witness in himself: he that believeth not God hath made him a liar; because he believeth not the record that God gave of his Son. And this is the record, that God hath given to us eternal life, and this life is in his Son. He that hath the Son hath life; and he that hath not the Son of God hath not life. These things have I written unto you that believe on the name of the Son of God; that ye may know that ye have eternal life, and that ye may believe on the name of the Son of God."
—1 JOHN 5:10–13

"For the which cause I also suffer these things: nevertheless I am not ashamed: for I know whom I have believed, and am persuaded that he is able to keep that which I have committed unto him against that day."—2 TIMOTHY 1:12

B. _____ *Power of the Holy Spirit*

- The new convert must understand that the Lord will keep him saved and the work of salvation is _____.

"In whom ye also trusted, after that ye heard the word of truth, the gospel of your salvation: in whom also after that ye believed, ye were sealed with that holy Spirit of promise."—Ephesians 1:13

II. _____

A. Baptism _____ *One with Christ*

- It is _____ on one's spiritual death to the old life and his newness of life in Christ.

"Know ye not, that so many of us as were baptized into Jesus Christ were baptized into his death? Therefore we are buried with him by baptism into death: that like as Christ was raised up from the dead by the glory of the Father, even so we also should walk in newness of life."—Romans 6:3–4

B. The _____ *of Early Christians*

- Christians in the early _____ were obedient to be baptized and were baptized soon after salvation.

- Baptism always _____ salvation.

"Then they that gladly received his word were baptized: and the same day there were added unto them about three thousand souls."—ACTS 2:41

"But when they believed Philip preaching the things concerning the kingdom of God, and the name of Jesus Christ, they were baptized, both men and women."—ACTS 8:12

C. The new _____ should desire to be _____.

"And as they went on their way, they came unto a certain water: and the eunuch said, See, here is water; what doth hinder me to be baptized?"—ACTS 8:36

D. True _____ is by _____.

"And Philip said, If thou believest with all thine heart, thou mayest. And he answered and said, I believe that Jesus Christ is the Son of God. And he commanded the chariot to stand still: and they went down both into the water, both Philip and the eunuch; and he baptized him. And when they were come up out of the water, the Spirit of the Lord caught away Philip, that the eunuch saw him no more: and he went on his way rejoicing."—ACTS 8:37–39

E. Building the _____ of the new Christian

- Baptism tells others that a person has accepted Christ as his personal Saviour.

F. Baptism is _____ to Christ.

- The desire of a soul winner should be to help a new convert get the right start in order to lay the _____ for a healthy Christian life.

"Whosoever therefore shall confess me before men, him will I confess also before my Father which is in heaven."—MATTHEW 10:32

G. How to be _____

1. The new convert should walk forward during the invitation.

2. A counselor will take the new convert to a changing room, complete with baptismal _____, towels, and hair dryers.

3. The counselor will give some _____ in how the baptism will be performed.

III. _____ _____

"Not forsaking the assembling of ourselves together, as the manner of some is; but exhorting one another: and so much the more, as ye see the day approaching." —HEBREWS 10:25

IV. Personal _____

"As ye have therefore received Christ Jesus the Lord, so walk ye in him: Rooted and built up in him,

and stablished in the faith, as ye have been taught, abounding therein with thanksgiving. Beware lest any man spoil you through philosophy and vain deceit, after the tradition of men, after the rudiments of the world, and not after Christ."—COLOSSIANS 2:6–8

A. Set aside a _____ time each day for systematic Bible study.

"All scripture is given by inspiration of God, and is profitable for doctrine, for reproof, for correction, for instruction in righteousness: That the man of God may be perfect, throughly furnished unto all good works."—2 TIMOTHY 3:16–17

B. Spend time in _____.

"Let us therefore come boldly unto the throne of grace, that we may obtain mercy, and find grace to help in time of need."—HEBREWS 4:16

V. The Importance of _____

A. Personal _____ is the key.

- Continue to fellowship with the new Christian until that person is grounded in the _____.

B. Fellowship with a _____

1. _____ about things which will be useful for spiritual edification.

2. Speak _____ of the church and of the pastoral staff.

3. Talk about the _____ of being a Christian.

4. Introduce the new Christian to other _____.

5. Have _____ with the new Christian who has not yet learned to control his vocabulary and habits.

6. Have the _____ in spotless condition.

7. Do not attempt to act as the pastor and have a mini-_____ service.

8. Do not fellowship with the same _____ repeatedly.

9. End the fellowship in _____ to God thanking Him for fellowship through Christ.

VI. The Importance of _____ _____

"Go ye therefore, and teach all nations, baptizing them in the name of the Father, and of the Son, and of the Holy Ghost: Teaching them to observe all things whatsoever I have commanded you: and, lo, I am with you alway, even unto the end of the world. Amen."
—MATTHEW 28:19–20

"And the things that thou hast heard of me among many witnesses, the same commit thou to faithful men, who shall be able to teach others also."—2 TIMOTHY 2:2

VII. Being an _____

- Three important steps to set the example for the new Christian.

A. Set the right _____.

"...*as ye know what manner of men we were among you for your sake.*"—1 THESSALONIANS 1:5B

B. The new Christian will _____ your example.

"*And ye became followers of us, and of the Lord....*"
—1 THESSALONIANS 1:6A

C. The new Christian will _____ an example.

"*So that ye were ensamples to all that believe in Macedonia and Achaia.*"—1 THESSALONIANS 1:7

Priorities of the Church

Introduction: _____
_____
_____

I. A Clearly Defined _____

A. *Committed to personal* _____
"Brethren, I count not myself to have apprehended:
but this one thing I do, forgetting those things which
are behind, and reaching forth unto those things
which are before."—PHILIPPIANS 3:13

B. *Establishing and refining clear* _____

II. _____ a Heart for God

A. *Ministries that* _____
"I will bless the LORD at all times: his praise shall
continually be in my mouth. My soul shall make her
boast in the LORD: the humble shall hear thereof,
and be glad. O magnify the LORD with me, and let
us exalt his name together."—PSALM 34:1–3

"Speaking to yourselves in psalms and hymns and
spiritual songs, singing and making melody in your
heart to the Lord."—EPHESIANS 5:19

B. The place of _____

"Preach the word; be instant in season, out of season;
reprove, rebuke, exhort with all longsuffering and
doctrine."—2 TIMOTHY 4:2

C. Supporting the pillar of _____

III. _____ People in the Church Family

"Then they that gladly received his word were baptized:
and the same day there were added unto them about
three thousand souls."—ACTS 2:41

"Now therefore ye are no more strangers and foreigners,
but fellowcitizens with the saints, and of the household
of God."—EPHESIANS 2:19

A. Included through _____

B. Included through _____

   1. The _____ ministry

   2. The _____ ministry

   3. _____

   4. Ministry _____

IV. _____ People from God's Word

A. Instructed through _____ **and**

_____

"And they continued stedfastly in the apostles' doctrine and fellowship, and in breaking of bread, and in prayers."—ACTS 2:42

"But be ye doers of the word, and not hearers only, deceiving your own selves."—JAMES 1:22

B. Instructed through personal _____

V. _____ **People in the Ministry of Christ**

"As every man hath received the gift, even so minister the same one to another, as good stewards of the manifold grace of God."—1 PETER 4:10

A. Each person has a _____ **in the body**

B. Protecting _____ *purity* **while maintaining** _____ *sensitivity*

C. Equipping the _____ *for the* **ministry**

VI. _____ **Your Region and Your World with the Gospel**

"But ye shall receive power, after that the Holy Ghost is come upon you: and ye shall be witnesses unto me both in Jerusalem, and in all Judaea, and in Samaria, and unto the uttermost part of the earth."—ACTS 1:8

A. *Saturation* _____

B. _____ *Personal Soul Winners*

C. *The _____ ministry*

D. *Special Sundays of* _____

E. *Community-Related* _____

F. *Five Priorities of Working Together*
   1. Inspire
   2. Include
   3. Instruct
   4. Involve
   5. Impact

Soul Winner's 10 Commandments

Commandment #1

Always be polite, courteous, and thoughtful of others.

Commandment #2

Always introduce yourself and the church immediately.

Commandment #3

Give each person a sincere invitation to visit our church and leave a brochure.

Commandment #4

Never be forceful, overbearing, or inconsiderate in any way.

Commandment #5

Never criticize another person's beliefs.

Commandment #6

Never talk alone in a house with a person of the opposite gender.

Commandment #7

Never talk to a child under thirteen years of age without a parent present.

Commandment #8

Always be apologetic and considerate if you interrupt sleep, meals, or other activities.

Commandment #9

Never be rude or verbally combative no matter what is said or how you are treated.

Commandment #10

Always be led by the Holy Spirit and be a good ambassador for your God and your church!

Leading a Soul to Christ

"The fruit of a Christian is another Christian."

Perhaps the greatest joy any Christian could experience is that of leading someone else to a saving knowledge of Jesus Christ. Second to that would be the joy of seeing that new Christian grow and tell others what God has done for him. John said that he had no greater joy than to hear that his children walked in truth. Soul winning is a path of truth—for only the truth can liberate a sin-enslaved lost man.

The simple truth below demonstrates the basic truths that any Christian should know in leading someone to Christ. May these simple truths become an integral part of your walk with God.

1. **God loves you.**
    "For God so loved the world, that he gave his only begotten Son, that whosoever believeth in him should not perish, but have everlasting life."
    —JOHN 3:16

2. **All men are sinners.**
    "For all have sinned, and come short of the glory of God."—ROMANS 3:23

3. **Sin must be paid for.**
    "For the wages of sin is death; but the gift of God is eternal life through Jesus Christ our Lord."
    —ROMANS 6:23

4. ***Christ paid for your sins.***
   "But God commendeth his love toward us, in that, while we were yet sinners, Christ died for us."
   —ROMANS 5:8

5. ***You must personally put your trust in Christ to save you.***
   "For whosoever shall call upon the name of the Lord shall be saved."—ROMANS 10:13

How to Be an Effective Soul Winner

1. **Pray for a burden.**
    "Lord, give me a burden for souls."

2. **Schedule a time for soul winning.**
    Spontaneously or organized

3. **Carry tracts with you.**

4. **Update your sweetheart list every week.**
    *   Pray, daily, for each person on your list.

    *   Contact each person weekly either by visit, phone or a note.

5. **Be attentive in the services.**

6. **Set goals for salvation plans presented.**

7. **Be hospitable.**

8. **Introduce potential converts to someone with common interests.**

9. **Find out who their unsaved friends are and try to reach each one with the Gospel.**

Using a Sweetheart List

I. How to Formulate a Sweetheart List...

A. *Door-to-door soul winning*

B. *Visitors from Sunday*

C. *Out and about—barber, grocery store, shopping, etc.*

D. *Friends or family members*

E. *Bus Ministry*

F. *New move-in visits*

II. What to do with a Sweetheart List...

A. *Look at it every day*

B. *Pray over it every day*

C. *Contact every person once a week (either by visit, phone or card)*

III. Who is on a Sweetheart List...

A. *Anyone unsaved*

B. *Anyone not baptized*

C. *Anyone who is not a member of the church*

IV. What is the Goal of a Sweetheart List...

A. *To see people saved*

B. *To see people baptized*

C. *To see people added to the church—(transfer of membership)*

V. When the Goal is Met, What is Next...

A. *Introduce them to other Christians*

B. *Make one or two follow-up visits*

C. *Have them over for fellowship*

D. *Give them follow-up materials*

E. *"Pastor" them*

F. *Promote loyalty to God, God's man, and the local church*

Sweetheart List

Soul Winning Sweetheart List   for the month of: _____

Name: _____ Phone #: _____

Address: _____ Zip: _____

Date										
Contact										

PH=phone call   C/N=card or note   V=personal visit

Comments: _____
_____

- -

Soul Winning Sweetheart List   for the month of: _____

Name: _____ Phone #: _____

Address: _____ Zip: _____

Date										
Contact										

PH=phone call   C/N=card or note   V=personal visit

Comments: _____
_____

- -

Soul Winning Sweetheart List   for the month of: _____

Name: _____ Phone #: _____

Address: _____ Zip: _____

Date										
Contact										

PH=phone call   C/N=card or note   V=personal visit

Comments: _____
_____